500. YIL VAKFI
"İNSANLIĞA ÖRNEK"

THE TURKISH JEWS
700 Years of Togetherness

Naim Avigdor GÜLERYÜZ

GÖZLEM

THE TURKISH JEWS
700 Years of Togetherness

Naim Avigdor Güleryüz

ISBN: 978 - 9944 - 994 -38-5
Certificate No: 12211

Book Design : Semra Sevinç
Cover Design : Bella Parlakşimşek
Cover : Composition with objects displayed at the Jewish Museum of Turkey

Photo Credits
İzzet Keribar : pp. 7, 39, 40, 44, 49, 50, 54, 56, 60, 63, 64
Don Halperin : pp. 12, 13

Express Grafik Baskı Sistemleri Matbaa ve Yay. San. Tic. Ltd. Şti.
Deposite İş Merkezi, A6 Blok, K.3, No. 309, Ikitelli-Istanbul
T: +90 (212) 671 61 51 F: +90 (212) 671 61 52

Gözlem Gazetecilik Basın ve Yayın AŞ
Atiye Sokak, Polar Apartmanı 12/6
Teşvikiye 34365 Istanbul-Türkiye
T: +90 (212) 231 92 82 F: +90 (212) 231 92 83
www.gozlemkitap.com

Preface

In 1991 I compiled *The History of the Turkish Jews*, a pocket booklet from different lectures I delivered on various US and European platforms as part of the commemoration of the warm welcome given by the Ottoman Empire to the Jews expelled from Spain and Portugal 500 years before. It was written primarily for foreigners visiting Turkey and those participating in the numerous international activities of the 500. Yıl Vakfı (Quincentenial Foundation), and summarised the history and social life of 700 years of peaceful co-existence of Jews with Muslims in Turkey.

After being reprinted in its original format several times, I have decided to enhance the content of the booklet with a new publication, which now includes information on Synagogues in Istanbul and Anatolia, commentary on the Ashkenazi and Karaite congregations, an introduction to the Jewish Museum of Turkey (Turk Musevileri Muzesi), Jewish sightseeing suggestions and a variety of photographic material. A selected bibliography has been incorporated for those interested in learning more about Turkish Jews.

I hope it will please you.

Naim Avigdor Güleryüz
November 2009, Istanbul

The Turkish Jews

Foreword

On the midnight of August 2nd 1492, when Columbus embarked on what would become his most famous expedition to the New World, his fleet departed from the relatively unknown seaport of Palos because the shipping lanes of Cadiz and Seville were clogged with Sephardic Jews expelled from Spain by the Edict of Isabella, Queen of Castile and Fernando, King of Aragon, signed at the Alhambra on March 31st, 1492.

The Jews were forced either *to convert to Catholicism or to leave the country* under menace *they dare not return... not so much as to take a step on them not trespass upon them in any manner whatsoever*. The great majority left their land, their property, their belongings all that was theirs and familiar to them, rather than abandon their beliefs, their traditions, their heritage. While most countries in Europe were reluctant to accept these refugees, in the faraway Ottoman Empire, one ruler extended an immediate welcome to those persecuted Jews, the Sephardim.[1] He was the Sultan Bayazid II.

In 1992, the Discovery Year for all those connected to the American continent - North, Central and South -, world Jewry was concerned with commemorating not only the expulsion, but also seven centuries of the Jewish life in Spain, and celebrating the 500th anniversary of the official welcome extended by the Ottoman Empire in 1492.

That year, Turkish Jewry celebrated not only the anniversary of this gracious welcome, but also the remarkable humanitarian spirit which has characterized the whole Jewish experience in Turkey. The events being planned - symposiums, conferences, concerts, exhibitions, films and books, restoration of ancient synagogues etc. - commemorated the longevity and prosperity of the Jewish community. As a whole, the celebration aimed to demonstrate the richness and security of life Jews have found in the Ottoman Empire and the Turkish Republic over seven centuries, and showed that indeed it is not impossible for people of different creeds to live together peacefully under one flag.

---

1 Sepharad is the Hebrew name for the Iberian Peninsula. But it's little known that the word Sepharad (Sfard) is found in the Holy Scriptures (Obadiah I:20) applied to (in the Aegian region of Anatolia, Turkey), as the site of a colony of exiles from Jerusalem, brought there by Zeuxis the viceroy of Antiochus III. This name was later applied to Spain. The descendants of Jews who lived in Spain and Portugal before their expulsion are called Sephardim (Encyclopedia Judaica,V.14, Keter Publishing House, Jerusalem)

Hanukiyyah Lamp,
in the shape of a Minaret

Jewish inscriptions and grafitti at *Aphrodisias* (probably 3rd century)
Courtesy of Cambridge Philologic Society, England

A History Predating 1492

It may be worthwhile to correct and clarify a persisting fallacy still assumed as true by many. 1492 was not the year when Jews first arrived to Turkey, but rather the year when the Sephardic Jews were welcomed in the Ottoman Empire.

The history of the Jews in Anatolia started many centuries before the migration of Sephardic Jews. Remnants of Jewish settlements from the 4th century B.C. have been uncovered in the Aegean region. The historian Josephus Flavius relates that Aristotle *met Jewish people with whom he had an exchange of views during his trip across Asia Minor.*[2]

Ancient synagogue ruins have been found in Sardes, Miletus, Priene, Phocee, etc. dating from 220 B.C. and traces of other Jewish settlements have been discovered near Bursa, in the southeast and along the Aegean, Mediterranean and Black Sea coasts. A bronze column found in Ankara confirms the rights the Emperor Augustus accorded the Jews of Asia Minor.

Jewish communities in Anatolia flourished and continued to prosper through the Turkish conquest. When the Ottomans captured Bursa in 1326 and made it their capital, they found a Jewish community oppressed under Byzantine rule. Sultan Orhan gave them permission to rebuild the *Etz Ahayim* (Tree of Life) Synagogue which remained in service until nineteen forties. The

2 Josephus Flavius, *Contra Apionem*, 1-176

Jews greeted the Ottomans as saviours.

Thus our commun history starts in fact in 1326, almost seven centuries ago.

Early in the 14th century, when the Ottomans had established their capital at Edirne, Jews from Europe, including Karaites, migrated there. Similarly, Jews expelled from Hungary in 1376, from France by Charles VI in September 1394, and from Sicily early in the 15th century found refuge in the Ottoman Empire. In the 1420's, Jews from Thesalonika, then under Venetian control, fled to Edirne.

Ottoman rule was much kinder than Byzantine rule had been. In fact, from the early 15th century on, the Ottomans actively encouraged Jewish immigration. Through a letter sent to Jewish communities in Europe in around 1454/1469, Yitshak Sarfati (Chief-Rabbi of Edirne) invited his co-religionists *to leave the torments they were enduring in Christianity and to seek safety and prosperity in Turkey.*[3]

When Mehmet II "the Conqueror" took Constantinople in 1453, he encountered an oppressed Romaniot (Byzantine) Jewish community which welcomed him with enthusiasm. Sultan Mehmet II issued a proclamation to all Jews ... *to ascend the site of the Imperial Throne, to dwell in the best of the land, each beneath his vine and his fig tree, with silver and with gold, with wealth and with cattle...*[4]

In 1470, Jews expelled from Bavaria by Ludwig X found refuge in the Ottoman Empire.

3 Bernard Lewis, *The Jews of Islam*, 135

4 Abraham Galante, *Histoire des Juifs dÎlstanbul*, V.1, 3

LETTER FROM RABBI YITSHAK SARFATI (*)

I have heard of the afflictions, more bitter than death, that have befallen our brethren in Germany – of the tyrannical laws, the compulsory baptisms and the banishments, which are of daily occurrence. I am told that when they flee from one place a yet harder fate befalls them in another. On all sides I learn of anguish, of soul and torment of body; of daily exactions levied by merciless oppressors. The clergy and monks, false priests that they are, rise up against the unhappy people of God. For this reason they have made a law that every Jew found upon a Christian ship bound for the East shall be flung into the sea. Alas! How evil are the people of God in Germany entreated; how sad is their strength departs! They are driven hither and thither, and they are pursued even unto death. Brothers and teachers, friends and acquaintances ' I, Yitshak Sarfati, though I spring from a French stock, yet I was born in Germany, and sat there at the feet of my esteemed teachers. I proclaim to you that Turkey is a land wherein nothing is lacking, and where if you will, all shall yet be well with you. The way the Holy Land lies open to you through Turkey. Is it not better for you to live under Muslims than under Christians? Here every man dwells at peace under his own wine and fig tree. Here you are allowed to wear the most precious garments. In Christendom, on the contrary, you dare not even venture to cloth your children in red or blue, according to your taste, without exposing them to insult or beaten black and blue, or kicked green and red, and therefore are you condemned to go about meanly clad in sad coloured raiment.. And now, seeing all these things, O Israel, wherefore sleepiest thou? Arise! And leave this accursed land forever!

(*) H. Graetz dates the letter approx. 1454

Remnants of *Sardes* Synagogue (3rd - 4th century)

Remnants of *Sardes* Synagogue (3rd - 4th century)

"Welcome", oil painting by Mevlut Akyıldız

Sultan Bayazid II (1447-1512)
8th ruler of the Ottoman Empire

1492 - A Haven for Sephardic Jews

Sultan Bayazid II's offer of refuge gave new hope to the persecuted Sephardim. In 1492, the Sultan ordered the governors of the provinces of the Ottoman Empire *not to refuse the Jews entry or cause them difficulties, but to receive them cordially.*[5] According to Bernard Lewis, *the Jews were not just permitted to settle in the Ottoman lands, but were encouraged, assisted and sometimes even compelled.*[6]

The arrival of the Sephardim altered the structure of the community and the original group of Romaniote Jews was totally absorbed.

Over the centuries an increasing number of European Jews, escaping persecution in their native countries, settled in the Ottoman Empire. In 1537 the Jews expelled from Apulia (Italy) after the city fell under Papal control, and in 1542 those expelled from Bohemia by King Ferdinand found a safe haven in the Ottoman Empire. In March of 1556, Sultan Suleyman "the Magnificent" wrote a letter to Pope Paul IV asking for the immediate release of the Ancona Marranos, which he declared to be Ottoman citizens. The Pope had no other alternative than to release them, the Ottoman Empire being the "Super Power" of those days.

---

5 M. Franco, *Essai sur l'Histoire des Israélites de l'Empire Ottoman, Depuis les origines jusquía nos jours*, 37

6 Bernard Lewis, *The Jews of Islam*, 138

By 1477, Jewish households in Istanbul numbered 1647 or 11% of the total. Half a century later, 8070 Jewish houses were listed in the city.

Jews fleeing the 1881, 1891, 1897 and 1902 pogroms in Russia and the 1917 Bolshevik Revolution also took refuge in Turkey.

EMIGRATION ROUTES

The Life of Ottoman Jews

For 300 years following the expulsion, the prosperity and creativity of the Ottoman Jews rivaled that of the Golden Age of Spain. With a Jewish population of almost 30,000, Istanbul thus became one of the most important Jewish centers of Europe. The Talmudic Academy that was established in Edirne, with the participation of many Sephardic philosophers, thinkers and scholars, trained students coming from all over Europe. Sfad (Safed) too became a world famous centre for religious philosophy and *Kabbalah*.

Iberian immigrants had to leave behind them all their fortunes and possessions. However, neither the kings of Spain nor the Mediterranean pirates were ever able to take away the qualifications and the talents of these people. At a time when the Ottoman State entered an era of great development, and as a consequence had a great need for qualified people, the Sephardic Jews, who were familiar with the arts, trade and techniques of medicine, printing, weaponry, textile weaving and dyeing, leather treatment and copper workmanship, contributed to their new homeland the expertise they had acquired in the Golden Age of Spain, during their cohabitation with Muslims and at times with Christians. The famous words attributed to Sultan Bayezid II, are worth remembering: *How can you call this king Fernando smart and sage?He is impoverishing his own country and enriching mine.*[7]

---

7 Immanuel Aboab, *Nomologia o Discursos Legales*

As a matter of fact, the first printing press in the Ottoman Empire was created in 1493 by the brothers David and Samuel ibn Nahmias, who had emigrated from Spain. Their first printed book, Jacob ben Asher's *Arba'ah Turim*, was printed on 13 December 1493.[8] Innovations in printing techniques such as italic type, page layout, folio numbering and the use of capital letters to mark the beginnings of paragraphs were all introduced in the 1530's by the Sonsino family who had arrived to Istanbul by way of Italy. More than forty books were printed by the Sonsinos between 1540 and 1547 and included a masterwork entitled *Multi Language Torah* (*Bible Polyglot*), printed in 1547. Between the beginning of the 16th and the end of the 18th centuries, Istanbul was one the main centers of Hebrew publishing.

Most of the court physicians were Jews: Hakim Yakoub, Joseph and Moshe Hamon, Daniel Fonseca, Gabriel Buenaventura to name only very few.

Number of Jews were assigned to distinguished posts in the Ottoman palace, especially in financial and foreign relations issues.

Ottoman diplomacy was often carried out by Jews. Joseph Nasi, appointed the Duke of Naxos, was the former Portuguese Marrano Joao Miques. Another Portuguese Marrano, Alvaro Mendes, was named Duke of Mytylene in return of his diplomatic services to the Sultan. Salomon ben Nathan Eskenazi arranged the first diplomatic ties with the British Empire. Jewish women such as Dona Gracia Mendes Nasi *La Seniora* and Esther Kyra exercised considerable influence in the Court.

In the free air of the Ottoman Empire, Jewish literature flourished. Joseph Caro compiled the *Shulhan Arouh*. Shlomo haLevi Alkabes composed the *Lekhah Dodi* a hymn which welcomes the Sabbath

---

8 Some scholars pretend there was an error reading the Hebrew numbers and that the printing year should be 1503

according to both Sephardic and Ashkenazi ritual. Jacob Culi began to write the famous *MeAm Loez.* Rabbi Abraham ben Isaac Assa became known as the father of Judeo-Spanish literature.

Jewish immigrants not only adapted themselves to their new home but also started to produce work identifying them with the new culture, the best examples of which are observed in the field of music. Numerous composers and musicians are still well-known to this day. Though the names of some are not known, their works are still played and listened to with great pleasure.

Prayers and hymns chanted on the religious days are composed with Turkish Music modes, e.g. *Isfahan* mode for the first two days of Passover and *Ajem-ashiran* for the last two days, *Mahur* mode for Shavuot, *Saba* mode for Purim, *Oushak* mode for Hanukkah.

Under Ottoman tradition, each non-Muslim religious community was responsible for its own institutions, including schools. In the early 19th century, Abraham de Camondo established a modern school, *La Escola*, causing a serious conflict between conservative and secular rabbis which was only settled by the intervention of Sultan Abdulaziz in 1864. The same year the *Takkanot haKehilla* (by-laws of the Jewish Community) was published, defining the structure of the Jewish community.

The Spanish and Portuguese refugees who immigrated to the Ottoman lands congregated in communities called *kehila*, that were usually divided into *kahals* designated by the names of the regions or towns they originated from. Every one of these *kahals* was independent and had its own synagogue, with its own rabbis, teachers, schools, religious institutions and charities and very often, their own religious tribunals. In the mid 16th century there were close to forty *kahal* only in Istanbul.

As to the Istanbul regions where the Istanbul Jews lived, at the time of Byzance Jews were mostly located in the *Halkoprateia* (Copper Dealers) district and that even as early as the year 318 a synagogue existed in this neighborhood. However, after Emperor Theodosius forbid them from residing in the city centre, they were resettled in the region called *Stenum* or *Stanyere*, on the northern shore of the Golden Horn estuary. As of the 9th century, Jews also lived on the southern shores of the Golden Horn, and mostly in the region between the Haghia Sophia and the present day Bahçekapı district. The entrance to this district in the city walls was situated not far from where the Yenicami Mosque now stands, and was called *Porta Iudece* (Jewish Door). From the 13th century until the conquest of Istanbul in 1453, Jews have lived especially in Langa and have engaged mostly with the leather business. According to edicts concerning the restoration of synagogues, in the late Byzantine era Jews lived also in the Balat region and on the Bosporus shores, at least in Ortaköy. As for Spanish immigrants, they were settled in Balat. At the time of the construction of the Yenicami Mosque in Eminönü, the Karaites who lived in these area were moved to Hasköy. Later Jews settled also on both sides of the Bosporus (Kuzguncuk, Dağhamamı, Beykoz on the Anatolian shore and Büyükdere, Yeniköy. Arnavutköy, Kuruçeşme on the European one).

At the beginning of the 20th century more affluent Jews began to settle in modern districts such as Taksim (Talimhane and Ayaspaşa), Şişli and Nişantaşı, while the others moved to the area around the Galata Tower. Nowadays there are no specific areas where the Jews of Istanbul live.

An important event in the life of Ottoman Jews in the 17th century was the schism led by *Sabetay Sevi*, the pseudo Messiah who lived in Izmir and later adopted Islam with his followers.

Me-am Loez
printed in Istanbul, 5493 (1732)

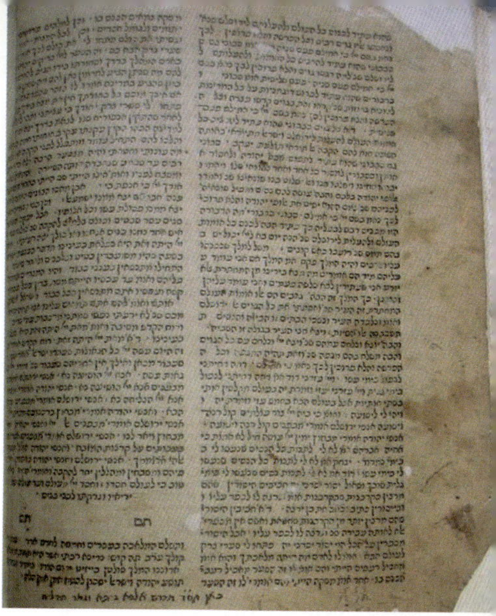

Midrash Teilim **(Interpretation of Teilim)**
printed in Istanbul 5272 (1511)

Milhemet Ahohma ve Aosher **(1543),**
Minhat Yehuda sone Anashim **(1543),** *Mihlol Yofi* **(1548),** *Zihron torat Moshe* **(1552)**

Sefer rosh Yosef **(1657),** *Sefer rosh Yosef 2* **(1657)**
Knesset Agedola **(1660)** *Netivot mishpat* **(1669)**

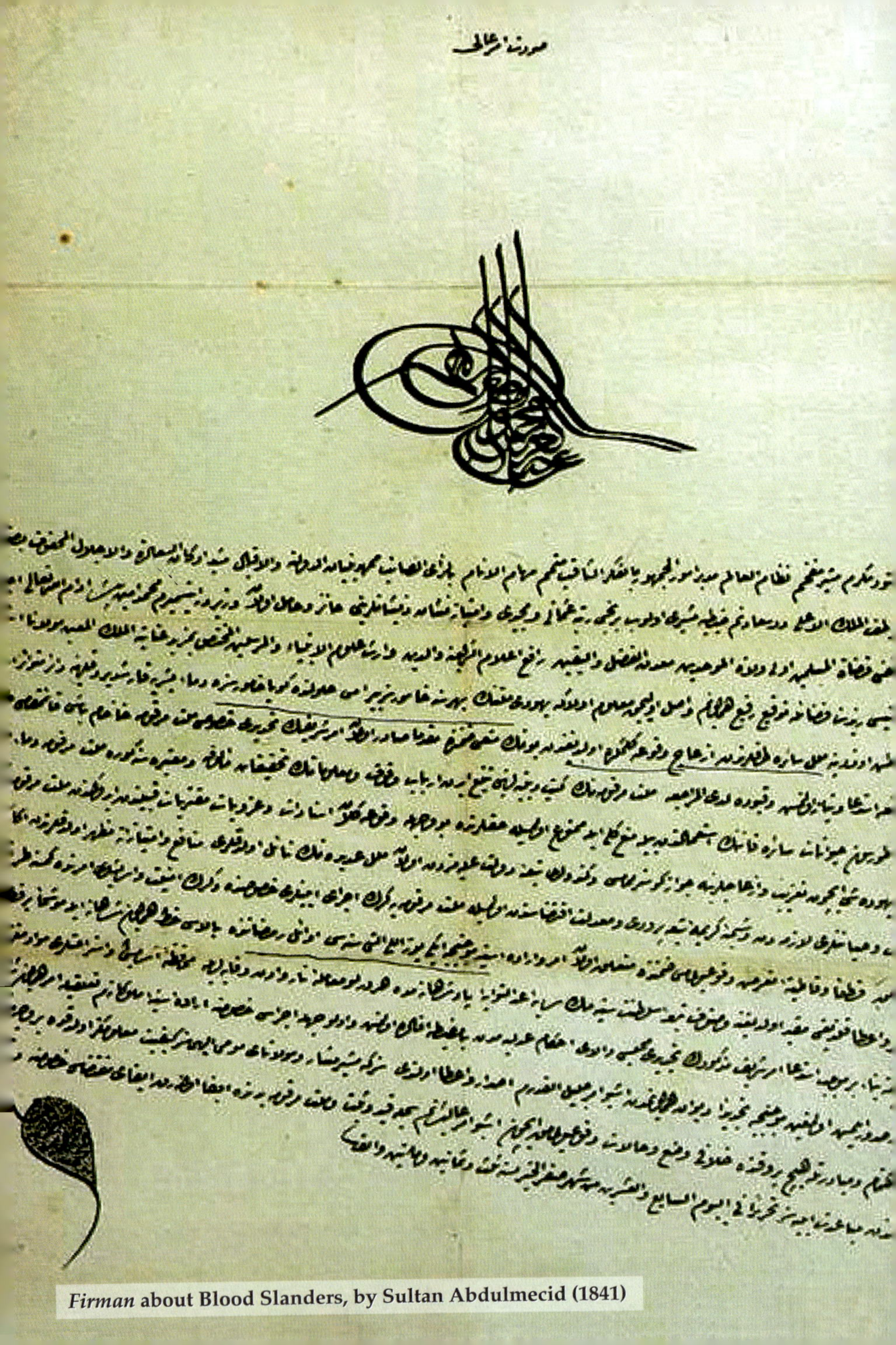

Firman about Blood Slanders, by Sultan Abdulmecid (1841)

Blood Libels and the Ottoman Sultans

Blood libels, which originated in the Middle Ages, accused Jews of using the blood of Christian children in the baking of their traditional unleavened bread, *matzoth*. In spite of explicit verses from the Bible, such as "*...therefore, I have said to the people of Israel: You shall not eat the blood of any creature, for the life of every creature is its blood; whoever eats it shall be cut off*" (Leviticus 17:14), these slanderous "myths" had the effect of inciting anti-Judaic beliefs and were, at least in part, responsible for the atrocities which were enacted upon the Jews of Europe in the period from 16th century to the end of the 19th century.

Following the blood libels in Amasya and Tokat, Suleyman the Magnificent ordered as follows:[9]

I would not like to see this millet's members attacked or treated unjustly. Such calumniation shall be dealt with only at the Sultan's Divan and nowhere else without my permission and consent.

The Ottoman Sultans issued a number of firmans about blood slanders. The firman by Sultan Abdulmecid (1841) following the events in Damascus and Rhodes in 1840, and the one by Sultan

9 Abraham Galante, *Documents Officiels Turcs concernant les Juifs de Turquie*, 15

Abdulaziz (1866) following the libel at Kuzguncuk in 1865 were put forward as strong evidence in various blood libel cases held in European courts.

On 27 October 1840 Sultan Abdulmecid issued his famous ferman on this subject saying:[10]

... and for the love we bear to our subjects, we cannot permit the Jewish nation, whose innocence for the crime alleged against them is evident, to be worried and tormented as a consequence of accusations which have not the least foundation in truth....

---

10 The original Firman is exhibited at the Jewish Museum of Turkey

Camondo Stairs, Galata - Istanbul

Mustafa Kemal Atatürk

End of the Ottoman Empire and the New Republic

Efforts at reform of the Ottoman Empire led to the proclamation of the *Hatt-ı Humayun* in 1856, which made all Ottoman citizens, Muslim and non-Muslim alike, equal under the law. As a result, leadership of the community began to shift away from the religious figure to secular forces. World War I brought to an end the glory of the Ottoman Empire. In its place rose the young Turkish Republic. Mustafa Kemal Atatürk was elected president, the Caliphate was abolished and a secular constitution was adopted.

Throughout the difficult days when Anatolia was under occupation[11], Turkish Jews in all occfupied areas kept their loyalty to the motherland and refused to collaborate with the occupying forces.[12]

Recognized in 1923 by the Treaty of Lausanne as a fully independent state within its present day borders, Turkey accorded minority rights to the three principal non-Muslim religious minorities and permitted them to carry on with their own schools, social institutions and funds.

On 15 September 1925, on the eve of Turkey's adoption of the Swiss

---

11 By British, Greek, French and Italian troops

12 Naim Güleryüz, *"Kurtuluş Savaşı'nda Türk Yahudileri"*, *Şalom*, January 11th, 2001

Civil Code, the leaders of the Jewish community meeting under the chairmanship of Rav Haim Becerano (Chief Rabbi *Locum Tenens*) prepared a petition, which they submitted to the Government and waived some of their rights acquired from the relevant articles of the Treaty of Lausanne (Chapter 3, Clause 42/2):

… As a result of the separation of religious and secular affairs, all laws are cleared of religion and prepared solely with respect to the requirements and the development of the state, thus rendering it unnecessary to have a special Jewish personal and family. ... Therefore, the Turkish Jews are willing to be subject to the secular laws that are issued in family and personal law as well as other fields of common law…

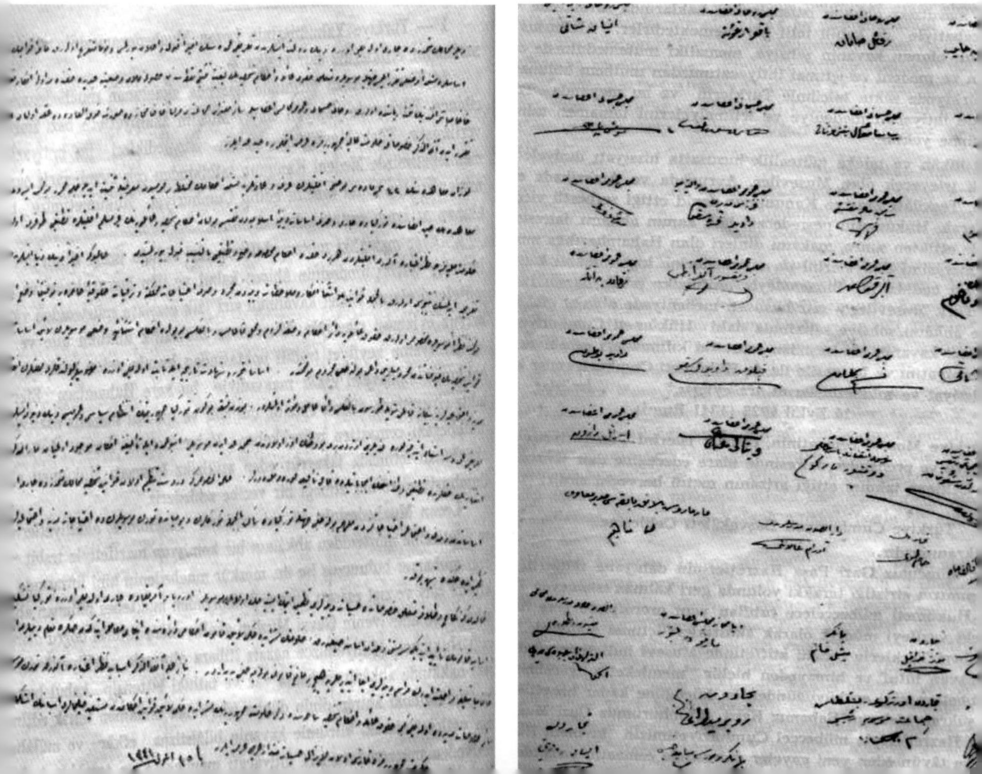

World War II

During the tragic days of World War II, Turkey managed to maintain its neutrality, by its chosen policy of *Peace at Home, Peace in the World*.

As early as 1933, when the first signs of a new world war appeared, Atatürk invited numbers of prominent German and Austrian scientists, mostly Jewish, to flee Nazi Germany and Austria, to find shelter in Turkey and continue their academic carriers at Turkish universities. Before and during the war years, these scholars contributed a great deal to the development of the Turkish university system.

During World War II Turkey served as a safe passage for many Jews fleeing the horrors of the Nazism. While the Jewish communities of Greece were wiped out almost completely by Hitler, the Turkish Jews remained secure.

Several Turkish diplomats, Ambassador Behiç Erkin, Consul-Generals Fikret Şefik Özdoğancı, Bedii Arbel, Selahattin Ülkümen; Consuls Namık Kemal Yolga and Necdet Kent, just to name only few, made every effort to save the Turkish Jews in the Nazi occupied countries, from the Holocaust. They succeeded. Mr. Selahattin Ülkümen, Consul General at Rhodes in 1943-1944, was recognized by the Yad-Vashem as a *Hassid Umot ha'Olam* (Righteous Gentile) in June 1990. Turkey continues to be a shelter, a haven for all those who have to flee dogmatism, intolerance and persecution.

Behiç Erkin, Ambassador of Turkey to Paris and Vichy (1940-1943)

Selahattin Ülkümen, Consul of Turkey in Rhodes (1943-1944)
***Hassid Umot ha'Olam*- Righteous Gentile**

Namık Kemal Yolga, Vice Consul in Paris (1942-1945) and Cevdet Dülger, Consul General in Paris (1939-1942)

Necdet Kent, Consul in Marseille (1942-1945)

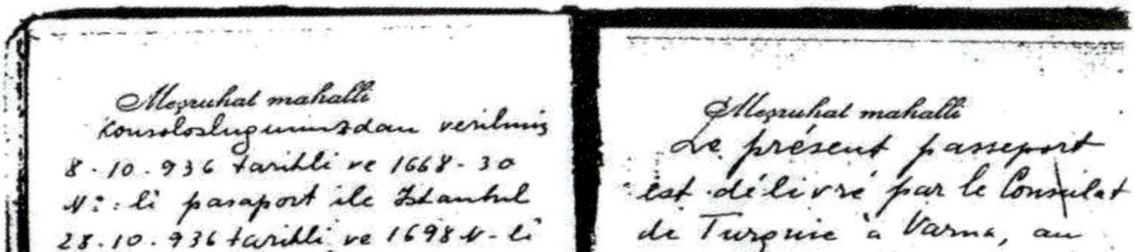

Meşruhat mahalli
Konsolosluğumuzdan verilmiş
8-10-936 tarihli ve 1668-30
N:li pasaport ile İstanbul
28-10-936 tarihli ve 1698 N-li
huruç kaydı ve en son 10.8.942
tarihinde temdit edilmiş 16.8.940
tarihli ve kütük 100, um. 414,
hususi 10 sayılı vatandaşlık
ilmühaberi üzerine verilmiş-
tir.

Varna, 5. 11. 942

№125344 *

Meşruhat mahalli
Le présent passeport
est délivré par le Consulat
de Turquie à Varna, au
citoyen Turc; Barouh Nessim
Lévi, pour se rendre en
Turquie.

Varna, le 5. 11. 1942
Le Consul de Turquie

125344 *

Chief Rabbi Raphael David Saban (1952-1960)

Chief Rabbi David Asseo (1961-2002)

Chief Rabbi Isak Haleva (2002-)

Turkish Jews Today

The present size of Jewish Community is estimated at around 20,000. The vast majority, almost 18,000 live in Istanbul, with a community of about 1,500 in Izmir and other smaller groups located in different towns like Adana, Ankara, Antakya, Bursa, Çanakkale, Kırklareli etc. Sephardim make up 96% of the Community, with Ashkenazim accounting for the rest. There are about less than 100 Karaites, an independent group who does not accept the authority of the Chief Rabbi.

Turkish Jews are legally represented, as they have been for many centuries, by the *Hahambasi*, the Chief Rabbi. He is assisted by a religious Council made up of five Hahamim. Fifty Lay Counsellors look after the secular affairs of the Community and an Executive Committee of fourteen runs the daily matters. Representatives of Jewish foundations and institutions meet four times a year as a so-called think tank, to exchange opinions on different subjects concerning the Turkish Jewry.

Most Jewish children attend state schools or private Turkish or foreign language schools. Many are enrolled in the universities. Additionally, the Community maintains in Istanbul a school complex including elementary and secondary schools for around 600 students. Turkish is the language of instruction, and Hebrew is taught 3 to 5 hours a week.

While younger Jews speak Turkish as their native language, the over-80-years-old generation is more at home speaking in French or

Judeo-Spanish (Ladino). A conscious effort is spent to preserve the heritage of Judeo-Spanish.

For many years Turkish Jews have had their own press. *La Buena Esperansa* and *La Puerta del Oriente* started in Izmir in 1843 and *Or Israel* was first published in Istanbul ten years later. Now, one newspaper survives: *Şalom (Shalom)*, a sixteen to twenty pages weekly in Turkish with one page in Judeo-Spanish (Ladino) and a 16-24 pages monthly supplement *El Amaneser*, also in Judeo-Spanish.

A Community Calendar (*Halila*) is published by the Chief Rabbinate every year and distributed free of charge to all those who have paid their dues (*Kisba*) to the welfare bodies. The Community cannot levy taxes, but accept donations.

Two Jewish hospitals, the 98 bed *Or-Ahayim* in Istanbul and the 22 bed *Karatas* Hospital in Izmir, serve the Community. Both cities have homes for the aged (*Moshav Zekinim*) and several welfare associations (*Matan Baseter*, Barınyurt, *Mishne Tora*) to assist the poor, the sick, the needy children and orphans.

Social youth clubs containing libraries, cultural and sports facilities, discotheques give young people the chance to meet and publish bi-monthly reviews covering a great variety of cultural articles.

And the first and only Jewish Museum of Turkey (www.muze500.com) has been inaugurated on November 2001.

The Jewish Community is of course a very small group in Turkey today, considering that the total population - 99% Muslim - exceeds 70 millions. But in spite of their number, the Jews have distinguished themselves. There are several Jewish professors teaching at the universities of Istanbul and Ankara, and many Turkish Jews are prominent in business, industry, almost all liberal professions and journalism.

Jewish school complex , Ulus - Istanbul

Weekly *Şalom* (since 1947) in Turkish and monthly *El Amaneser* in Judeo-Spanish

Kal Kadosh Agadol Synagogue, Edirne (in 1961)

The Synagogues of Anatolia

The existence in Anatolia of a multitude of Jewish settlements is confirmed not only by various historians and through archaeological excavations, but also by the large number of passages in the New Testament, related to the travels of the Apostles in Asia Minor and their efforts to convert Jews to Christianity. There are various theories on the arrival of Jews in Anatolia: they may have come from Mount Ararat, following the *Deluge*, or from Urfa after the Prophet Abraham (*Avraham Avinou*); they may have settled here for trading purposes; they may have been taken captive in Palestine by the Romans and settled here by force. They were members of about two thousand Jewish families known to have settled in the Lydian and Phrygian regions after having been forcibly moved from Babylonia in 202 B.C., by the Seleucian King Antiochos. Whatever their origin, Jews seem to have settled in the Aegean regions, mainly in towns such as Edremit, Bergama, Smyrna, Ephesus, Ödemiş, Sardes, Milet, Foça etc. and also in various parts of Asia Minor such as Bursa, Ankara, Konya, Cappadocia, Amasya, Tokat, Samsun, Tarsus, Urfa, Gaziantep, Van and the like, from the 4th century B.C. onwards.

The Milet Synagogue dating from the 3rd or 4th century A.D., discovered during an excavation by German archaeologists, the synagogue in Priene dating from the 4th or 5th century, and the ancient synagogue of Sardes which seems to have already existed somewhere between the 4th or 2nd century B.C. but had to be rebuilt after an earthquake in the 1st century A.D., are some of the oldest known synagogues of Anatolia to have survived from the classical ancient Jewish settlement system consisting of a community and a synagogue.

According to an inscription that was unearthed in 1875 and which later was lost, an ancient synagogue is said to have once existed also in Foça.

The Sardes Synagogue discovered during the excavations of 1960, has been restored and is now open to visitors. Among the synagogues that once existed in Anatolia and in Rumelia and which have survived to our day, are still in use: Musa in Kırklareli, Mekor Hayim in Çanakkale, Gerush and Mayor in Bursa, synagogues in Ankara, Adana, Iskenderun and Antakya and finally, the Beth Israel, Shaar Ashamayim, Bikur Holim, La Sinyora, Shalom, Rosh Aar and Algazi Synagogues in Izmir.[13]

---

13 For detailed information: Naim Güleryüz, *The Synagogues of Turkey*, jointly with İzzet Keribar for the photos, Gözlem Gazetecilik Basın ve Yayın A.Ş., Istanbul, 2008; Naim Güleryüz, *Dünden Bugüne Türkiye Sinagogları ve Bazı Kurumları*, (under printing)

Gerush Synagogue, Bursa

Shalom Synagogue, Izmir

Wedding ceremony at *Neve Shalom* Synagogue, Galata - Istanbul

The Synagogues of Istanbul

The first synagogue known to have existed in Istanbul was built in 318 in the *Halkoprateia* (Copper Dealers) district of the town. It was transformed into a church in 450 (442 according to Theopharos) by the Byzantine Emperor Theodosius II.

Entries on Sultan Mehmet the Conqueror's Register of Waqfs currently kept in the Treasury Section of the Topkapı Palace, refer to a synagogue that existed in the Copper Dealers Market (*Soukh el-Nahassin* or Bakırcılar), in the vicinity of Tahtakale.

Furthermore, in the same document is listed the presence of a synagogue in the Istanbul Halil Paşa Birgo district (the Bahçekapı neighborhood of our day) around 1455. From an Imperial Edict dated 15 Ramazan 1104 (21 May 1693) we note that three synagogues (Ahrida, Karaferya and Yanbol) dating from pre-conquest times existed in the Balat Hacı Isa district and yet another one (Çakacı or Çuhacı) in the Hasköy Tahta Minare quarter.

The remains of the oldest synagogue in the Galata district consist of a few stone lintels bearing Hebrew inscriptions discovered in the course of excavation work conducted in 1934 in the courtyard of the Galata Yenicami Mosque, which was built in 1697, behind the area where the Ottoman Bank now stands. It is believed that these remains belong to a synagogue that existed in this spot before the 17th century.

The synagogues of Istanbul show no characteristic architectural styles of their own: most were built in accordance with the tradition of their times or of the regions from which their builders originated. Synagogues built and restored after the 17th century were often influenced by Ottoman architecture (for example, the Ahrida Synagogue). 20th century synagogues show Moorish and Orientalist influences drawn from 19th century European style[14] (for example the Edirne, Büyükada, Yüksekkaldırım Ashkenazi synagogues). The natural disasters these synagogues have experienced, as well as the repairs, restorations and reconstructions they have undergone throughout the centuries have created obvious style differences, sometimes even within the same building. The renovation of the Ahrida Synagogue – which was disapproved of by the older generation in Balat – created a synagogue that is totally different from its pre-restoration appearance, but looks like it probably had been in the 17th century.

In Turkey, synagogues are classified as religious foundations (Vakifs). There are 20 active synagogues in Istanbul today: Balat Ahrida, Balat Yanbol, Sirkeci Hesed Beth Avraam, Sirkeci Çorapçı Han, Bakırköy, Caddebostan, Haydarpaşa Hemdat Israel, Kuzguncuk Beth Yaakov, Kuzguncuk Beth Nisim, Yeniköy Tiferet Israel, Ortaköy Etz Ahayim, Şişli Beth Israel, Galata Neve Shalom, Galata Italian (Kal de los Frankos), Yüksekkaldırım Ashkenazi, Hasköy Maalem and Kemerburgaz Shaar Ashamayim Synagogues. Three of them, Büyükada Hesed le Avraam, Heybeliada Beth Yaakov and Burgazada Ohel Yaakov, are in service for the summer season only.

Some of them are very old, especially Ahrida Synagogue in the Balat area, which dates from middle 15th century. The 15th and 16th century Hasköy and Kuzguncuk cemeteries in Istanbul are still in

---

14 Turgut Saner, *19. yüzyıl İstanbul Mimarlığında Oryantalizm*, Pera Turizm Yayınları, Istanbul, 1998

use today.

Two of non active synagogues have been assigned new functions. The Ashkenazi Tofre Begadim (Schneidertempel) which as of May 1999 has been in use as the *Schneidertempel Art Center* of the *Dr. Marcus Arts and Culture Association*, and the Kal Kadosh Zülfaris Synagogue in Karaköy, which was renovated by the 500. YıI Vakfı (*The Quincentennial Foundation*) and was opened in November 2001 as the 500. Yıl Vakfı Türk Musevileri Müzesi (*The Quincentennial Foundation Museum of Turkish Jews*, or shortly *The Jewish Museum of Turkey*).[15]

---

15 See footnote no.13 (p. 38)

Ashkenazi Synagogue, Yüksekkaldırım - Istanbul

Ashkenazi Jews

Ashkenazi Jews (*Ashkenazim*) were first seen in the Ottoman Empire in the second half of the 14th century, and their migration continued throughout the next centuries. Those who were expelled from Bohemia by King Ferdinand, those who managed to escape from the Bogdan Kmielnitzki (Chmielnicki) massacre in 1650, and others who fled the Crimean town of Kertch during the Crimean War found peace in the Ottoman lands.

However in time, due to differences in their cultural backgrounds, dissensions began to appear between the Ottoman Sephardim and the Ashkenazim, who would not recognize the authority of the local Chief Rabbi, and separate communities started forming even within the Ashkenazim themselves. Following lengthy discussions, an official agreement consisting of ten articles, duly stamped with the Chief Rabbi's seal, was signed on 1 Tammuz 5650, (June 19th 1890) between the Chief Rabbi and the representatives of the various Ashkenazi communities. According to this agreement, the Ashkenazim would henceforth form a single community with a board, a community president and rabbis who would enjoy the same *mare-de-atra* rights and powers as those of the other communities.

On 26 January 1912, the Ashkenazim who had convened on the initiative of Dr. Marcus, signed with the Chief Rabbinate a new eight article charter intended to replace the 1890 agreement. According to this agreement all the Ashkenazi congregations would unite under a single board or *hachgaha* that would be attached to the Chief

Rabbinate from a religious and administration point of view.

Official documents of 1954 refer to this community as "Jewish Ashkenazi Community"; but in 1957, the name was changed to the "Council of Trustees for the Jewish Ashkenazi Community's Yüksekkaldırım, Tofre Begadim and Or Hodesh Synagogues" and, after 1962, to the "Yüksekkaldırım Ashkenazi Jewish Synagogue Foundation – formerly the Jewish Ashkenazi Community".

According to the *Die Juden der Türkei* book by David Trietsch, over ten thousand Ashkenazi Jews lived in Istanbul in 1925. This figure has fallen today to under 600.

The Ashkenazi community owns a cemetery on the Arnavutköy hills (the actual Adnan Saygun boulevard), on land that was acquired in 1907 and whose use as a cemetery was authorized by a decree dated 1919. Of the three Ashkenazi synagogues of Istanbul only one, the Yüksekkaldırım Synagogue, is currently in use. Of the other two, the building of Or Hadash was sold and Tofre Begadim has become the Schneidertempel Arts Centre.[16]

16 See footnote no.13 (p. 38)

The Karaites

The word "Karaite" derives from the Hebrew word *kara* (to read) and means "those who read the *Torah*". The Karaites are also known as *Baalei la Mikra* (Owners of the *Torah*) or *Bnei ha Mikra* (Children of the *Torah*).

The Karaites apply only the plain meaning of the *Torah* text; they reject the later interpretations given by the rabbis or sages in the *Talmud*. Inspired by Prophet David's words *Oh God! I am calling you from the bottomless depths*, the Karaites build their synagogues, called *Ka'al* or *Kenessa*, under the ground level.

Benjamin de Tudela, the renowned traveller who visited Istanbul in 1172, wrote that there were some 500 Karaites living in the city at the time. According to Sultan Mehmet the Conqueror's Vakfiye (*Register of Pious Institutions*), the areas of Karaite settlement ranged from Eminönü-Balıkpazar and Balat, to Edirnekapı and the shores of Galata, that is, Karaköy. In fact, it is claimed that the name of Karaköy is an abbreviation of the expression "Karay Köy" (or Karaite Village). The researcher S. Şişman reports that a *kenessa* once existed at the junction of the Karaköy and Necati Bey Avenues. The synagogue of the Karaites who lived in Bahçekapı is believed to have been situated on the Arpacılar Street. As the Yenicami Mosque was constructed on ground partly belonging to the Karaites, the community was paid a yearly rent amounting to 2660 Akçe (Aspres) by the Imperial Treasury.

Today this community is independent of the Chief Rabbi and it has no clergy or religious authority. Their house of worship, *Ka'al Ha Kadosh Be Kushta Bene Mikra* in Hasköy date from Byzantine times but its exact date of construction is not known. The Karaites constitute an independant community known as the Turkish Karaite Community Foundation.[17]

17 See footnote no.13 (p. 38)

Ka'al Ha Kadosh Be Kushta Bene Mikra Karaite Synagogue, Hasköy - Istanbul

The Jewish Museum of Turkey, Istanbul (main hall)

The Jewish Museum of Turkey, (view from the women gallery - azara)

The Jewish Museum
500. Yıl Vakfı Türk Musevileri Müzesi

The Jewish Museum of Turkey has been established by the Quincentennial Foundation in the former Zulfaris Synagogue (*Kal Kadosh Galata*) situated in the Karaköy district of Istanbul, not far of the Golden Horn shore.

It aims to promote the story of 700 years of amity between Turks and Jews, beginning with the Ottoman conquest of Bursa (1326), to show through the past seven centuries how the two cultures influenced each other, and to display the humanitarian spirit of the Turkish Nation.[18] The Museum mission is to collect, preserve, and exhibit, interpret and disseminate knowledge about the cultural heritage of the Turkish Jews.

There is evidence that this synagogue existed in 1671. However the actual building was erected over its original foundations presumably in the early 19th century. The Zulfaris Synagogue remained in service until Jews living in the area moved to other neighbourhoods, around 1985. Then it has been assigned to the Quincentennial Foundation

---

18 During long centuries Turkey has been a land of refuge not only for Jews, but with no distinction of race or religion for all who had to flee the bigotry, the persecution, the religious intolerance. For more detailed information: *They Had Faith in Turkey,* Ministry of Foreign Affairs, Ankara 2006, Exhibition Catalogue

who restored the building as a Museum, not amending its synagogue appearance.

The Museum has been possible with the financial backing of the Kamhi Family and the valuable contributions of Jak Kamhi (Honorary President of the Foundation) and thanks to the vision and dedication of Naim Avigdor Güleryüz (President).

The exhibition in the Main Hall explores, through objects, documents and photos, the cultural heritage of Turkish Jews, their common life and interaction with the Muslim majority, their contribution to the social, intellectual and political life of the country. In the *Azara* (former women's gallery), photos are displayed and case stories depicted. On the ground floor, arranged as an Ethnographic Section, inheritance becomes cultural heritage. Through scenes such as birth and circumcision, trousseau and wedding, this section summarizes the customs of Turkish Jews and explores the influence of the broader society.

The display concept is intended to be dynamic, case stories change from time to time and temporary exhibitions organised.

The Museum is opened from Monday to Thursday (10:00 to 16:00), Friday and Sunday (10:00 to 14:00), but is closed on Saturdays and High Holidays.

Tzedakah **Box (Alms Box), dated 1912**
from the ***Balat Lounge Synagogue*****, Istanbul**

Tallid **dated 5658 (1898)**
original in New York

Hemdat Israel Synagogue, Haydarpaşa - Istanbul

Conclusion

Istanbul... The city that has been the capital of two big empires: East Roman & Ottoman. Laying on two continents Istanbul is situated at the crossroads between east and west, in an area where Europe meets Asia. Thus Turkey creates a bridge and a link between these two civilizations.

But, Istanbul is also the only city where mosques, synagogues and churches have stood side by side – in continuous use - in harmony – for seven centuries.

This humanitarianism demonstrated at that time, was consistent with the beneficence and goodwill traditionally displayed by the Turkish government and people towards those of different creeds, cultures and backgrounds. Indeed, Turkey could serve as a model to be emulated by any nation which finds refugees from any of the four corners of the world standing at its doors.

Schneidertempel Art Center (former *Ashkenazi* Synagogue), Galata - Istanbul

Suggestions for Jewish Sightseeing in Istanbul

First Day

- The Galata Tower neighborhood, a former Jewish district
- The vicinity of the Galata Tower
  - Neve Shalom Synagogue*
  - Italian Synagogue (Kal de los Frankos)*
  - Yüksekkaldırım Ashkenazi Synagogue*
  - Schneidertempel Art Center,
  - Camondo Stairs and Residence,
  - Jewish Museum of Turkey (www.muze500.com)

Second Day

could be combined with visits to Sultan Ahmed (Blue Mosque), Ayasofya (Hagia Sophia) Mosque, Underground Cistern (Yerebatan Sarayı), Covered Bazaar (Kapalıçarşı)

- The Golden Horn (Halic)
  - The Elderly Home (Hasköy)*
  - The Or Ahayim Jewish Hospital (Balat)*
  - The Ahrida and/or Yanbol Synagogues (Balat)*

Third Day

could be combined with visits to Dolmabahçe Sarayı, Ortaköy Camii, Beylerbeyi Sarayı

- Nişantaşı
- Cultural Center of Ottoman-Turkish Researches
- Etz Ahayim Synagogue (Ortaköy)*
- Ortaköy Square and vicinity
- Crossing the Bosphorus by boat to the Anatolian Shore
- Beth Yaakov Synagogue (Kuzguncuk)*
- Kuzguncuk Cemetary *

Fourth Day *(in spring, summer and autumn)*

- Büyükada Island, by ferry boat

Important: To attend the places marked (*) you need to get a permission from the Chief Rabbinate, prior to your visit. At this end, you will have to address to *info@musevicemaati.com*, indicating the schedule of your stay, the places you intend to visit and attach a copy of your passport identity and validity pages.

Ceremony hold at the former *Kal Kadosh Galata* (*Zulfaris* Synagogue), now the Jewish Museum of Turkey, commemorating Jewish martyrs during the Crimean War (1856) *"L'Illustration"*, Paris, September 13th, 1856, No. 103

rayer offered at the *Ahrida* Synagogue, for the victory of the Ottoman Army on th war against Russia, with the presence of the Sadrazam (Prime Minister) Ibrahim Edhem Pasha (May 1877) *"The Illustrated London News"*, London, June 9th, 1877, No. 541

Kal Kadosh Agadol Synagogue, Edirne

Selected Bibliographia

Aboab, Immanual - *Nomologia o Discursos Legales*, Portugal

Barnai, Jacob - *"Organization and Leadership in the Jewish Community of Izmir in the Seventeenth Century" The Jews of the Ottoman Empire,* editor Avigdor Levy, The Darwin Press Inc., Princeton, 1994

Benbassa, Esther - *Un Grand Rabbin Sépharade en politique 1892-1923*, Presses de CNRS, Paris, 1990

Epstein, Mark Alan - *The Ottoman Jewish Communities and their role in the Fifteenth and Sixteenth Centuries,* Klaus Schwarz Verlag, Freiburg, 1980

Franco, M. - *Essai sur l'Histoire des Israélites de l'Empire Ottoman, Depuis les origines jusqu'a nos jours*, Librairie A. Dublacher, Paris, 1897

Galante, Abraham - *Histoire des Juifs de Turquie*, 9 volumes, Isis, Istanbul, 1986

Galante, Abraham - *Documents Officiles concernant les Juifs de Turquie*, Istanbul, 1931

Graetz, Heinrich - *History of the Jews*. v. IV, 1894, Philadephia, 1949

Güleryüz, Naim - *İstanbul Sinagogları*, Ajans Class Reklamcılık Yayıncılık, Istanbul, 1992

Güleryüz, Naim - *Türk Yahudileri Tarihi-I (20. yüzyılın başına kadar)*, Gözlem Gazetecilik Basın ve Yayın AŞ, Istanbul, 1993

Güleryüz, Naim - *"Kurtuluş Savaşı'nda Türk Yahudileri"*, Şalom, January 11th, 2001

Güleryüz, Naim - *500. Yıl Vakfı Türk Musevileri Müzesi Albümü, The Quincentennial Foundation Museum of Turkish Jews Album*, Gözlem Gazetecilik Basın ve Yayın AŞ, Istanbul, 2004

Güleryüz, Naim - *"Osmanlı'da İlk Basımevi, Yahudi Matbaacılığı"*, Toplumsal Tarih, December 2006, 46-52

Güleryüz, Naim - *The Synagogues of Turkey*, jointly with İzzet Keribar for the photos, Gözlem Gazetecilik Basın ve Yayın AŞ, Istanbul, 2008

Güleryüz, Naim - *Dünden Bugüne Türkiye Sinagogları ve Bazı Kurumları*, (under printing)

Levy, Avigdor - *The Sephardim in the Ottoman Empire*, The Darwin Press Inc., Princeton, 1992

Levy, Avigdor - *The Jews of the Ottoman Empire*, The Drawin Press Inc., Princeton, 1994

Lewis, Bernard - *The Jews of Islam*, Princeton University Press, New Jersey, 1984

Reisman, Arnold - *Turkey's Modernization, Refugees from Nazism and Ataturk's Vision*, New Academia Pubisher, USA, 2006

Rodrigue, Aron - *French Jews Turkish Jews*, Indiana University Press, 1990

Saner, Turgut - *19. Yüzyıl İstanbul Mimarlığında Oryantalizm*, Pera Turizm Yayınları, Istanbul, 1998

Shaw, Stanford J. - *The Jews of the Ottoman Empire and the Turkish Republic*, New York University Press, New York, 1991

Shaw, Stanford J. - *Turkey and the Holocaust*, Palgrave Macmillan, UK, 1993

Türkoğlu, İnci - *Antik Çağ'dan Günümüze Türkiye'de Sinagog Mimarisi*, Ege Üniversitesi Sosyal Bilimler Enstitüsü Sanat Tarihi Anabilim Dalı, Izmir, 2001 (thesis not yet published)